FUNKY FABRICS OF THE 60S

Joy Shih

Schiffer Publishing Ltd

77 Lower Valley Road, Atglen, PA 19310

DEDICATION

To my husband, Don, for sharing the 60s experience with me,
and our children, Greg and Lauren, for continuing the "spirit" into the next generation.
We tried so hard to be a cool family.

Printed in Hong Kong
ISBN: 0-7643-0174-8

Library of Congress Cataloging-in-Publication Data

Shih, Joy.
    Funky fabrics of the 60s / Joy Shih.
        p.   cm.
    ISBN 0-7643-0174-8
      1. Textile fabrics--United States--History--
20th century Themes, motives.   I. Title.
NK8812.S56 1996
746'.0973'09046--dc20   96-9354
                             CIP

Published by Schiffer Publishing Ltd.
77 Lower Valley Road
Atglen, PA 19310
Telephone 610-593-1777
Fax 610-593-2002
Please write for a free catalog.
This book may be purchased from the publisher.
Please include $2.95 for shipping.
Try your bookstore first.

We are interested in hearing from authors
with book ideas on related subjects.

CONTENTS

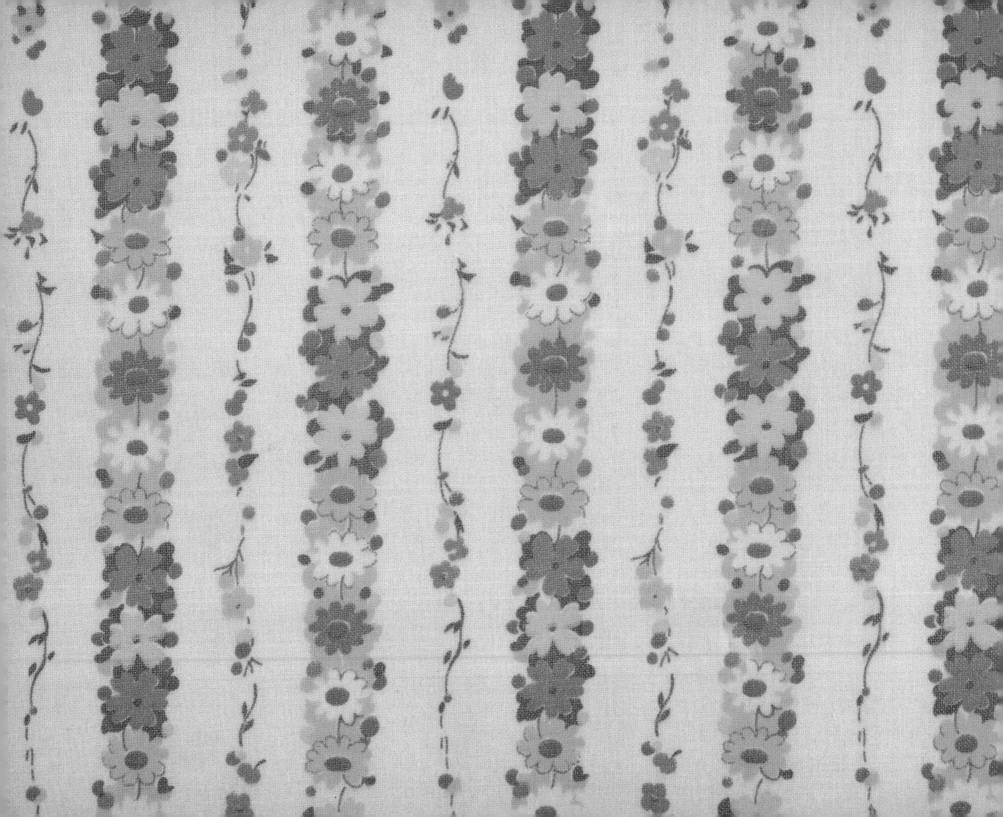

INTRODUCTION

The 1960s was a decade of significant changes. With advanced technological capabilities, notably in the area of communication, the world became a much smaller place. Events happening around the globe became news overnight. World leaders worked together at the United Nations. Pop culture transcended national borders and crossed oceans. Americans, with spirits buoyed by the election in 1960 of a new and much younger president, John F. Kennedy, were ready for fresh ideas. The young, beautiful, and sophisticated new First Lady, Jackie Kennedy, set a fashion trend for post-war babies now coming of age in a decade that would forever revolutionize American culture.

Textile designs in the 60s reflected the transition from the previous decade. Futuristic themes prevalent in 1950s designs were now, in essence, a reality with space exploration programs. Modern streamlined kitchen appliances and gadgets, no longer a novel idea, were now in use in most people's homes. Perhaps in reaction to all the technology and chrome, people felt a need to return to nature. Fabric designs in the early part of the decade responded with a new appreciation for earth tones of brown, green, gold and orange. Pinks and blues appeared in darker and more intense hues, particularly in floral prints. Kitchens across America began to take on a "homier" feel with warm images of spice racks, canisters, casseroles, and breads. Early American furniture with its warm "rustic" feel appeared in rec rooms and dens, along with drapes featuring Americana themes. In the bedroom, however, pastel shades dominated in printed pillowcase designs, especially early in the decade when people still made their own pillowcases.

By mid-decade, the assassination of President Kennedy in 1963, the harsh realities of war in Vietnam, poverty, and racial unrest awakened Americans to very real problems beyond the comforts of suburban homes and the simple lives portrayed by television "sitcom" families. Baby-boom children growing up found a whole new, ever-changing world, brought home in living color on nightly television news programs. Protesters of war and injustice countered dark

5

violence with bright flowers as symbols of peace and love. Teenagers eager to break free from their sugar-coated childhoods escaped into a world of sexual freedom, folk and rock music, organic gardening, Eastern religions, and peasant culture. Thus the "flower children" were born.

Though florals have historically been a strong theme in fabric design, flowers really took off in the 60s. Gone were fussy designs mixed with strange geometric shapes, wild abstracts, and bold hothouse florals favored in the last decade. Designers in the first half of the 1960s began moving from abstracts to smaller and unassuming prints, in neater, more orderly, patterns. Pastels fashionable in the 50s were substituted with darker and more "earthy" colors in the 60s. Calico, patchwork, and bandanna prints were popular during the period, often appearing in "peasant-type" clothing worn by young people. The drug and music culture prevalent later in the decade brought with it florals in shocking psychedelic and neon colors. One can almost follow the popular trends of the 60s from beginning to end simply by observing color and style changes in floral patterns. Note the color changes from darker tones in the early years, to lighter and brighter hues in mid-decade, and finally to "hot" shades in late decade. To help you appreciate these changes, the floral de-

signs in this book, in their sub-categories, have been arranged chronologically.

Other noticeable design changes from the previous decade include a move away from stereotypical "ethnic" images to a more sophisticated world view. The lack of designs in this category says it all. Instead of exotic destinations, generic architectural patterns followed. "Ethnic" images were replaced by elemental designs using geometric patterns as seen in Indian-inspired paisley prints. Geometrics were no longer simple stripes, checks, plaids, and polka dots, though these were still available, but complicated designs using combinations of shapes arranged in diverse geometric patterns. A decrease in children's designs and those featuring cowboy heroes probably followed the decline in the birth rate and the demise of television westerns. Children's patterns now featured cute animals in "baby" pastel colors. Youth trends also created an interest in denims.

The fabric designs in this book are taken from numerous volumes of 1960s textile manufacturers' sample pattern books. For baby boomers like me, this "trip" back offers many memories of a time best remembered for its "funky" spirit.

FLOWER POWER

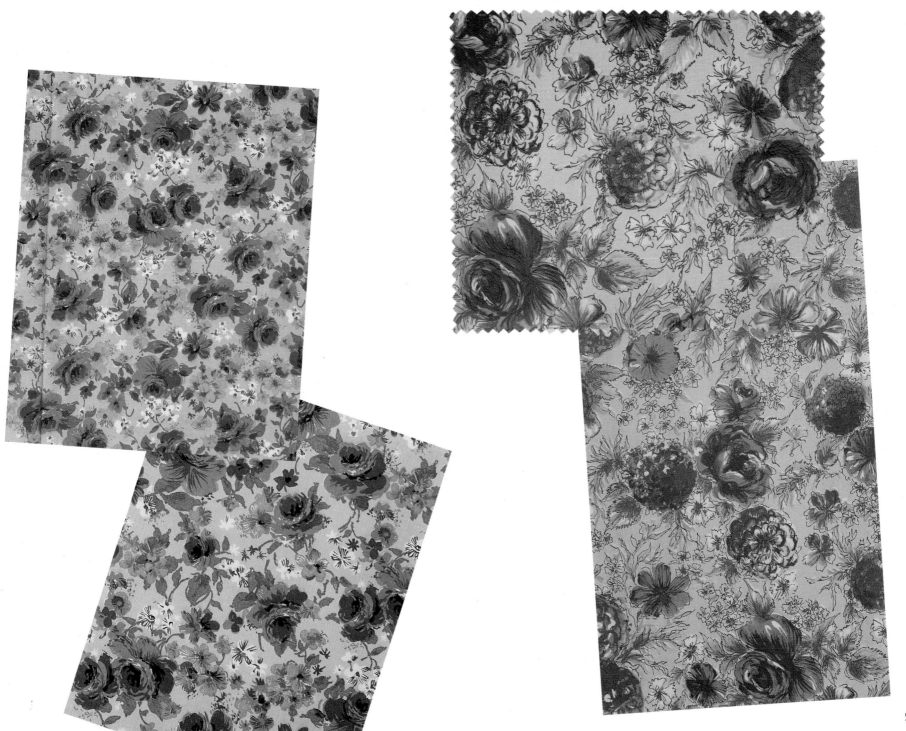

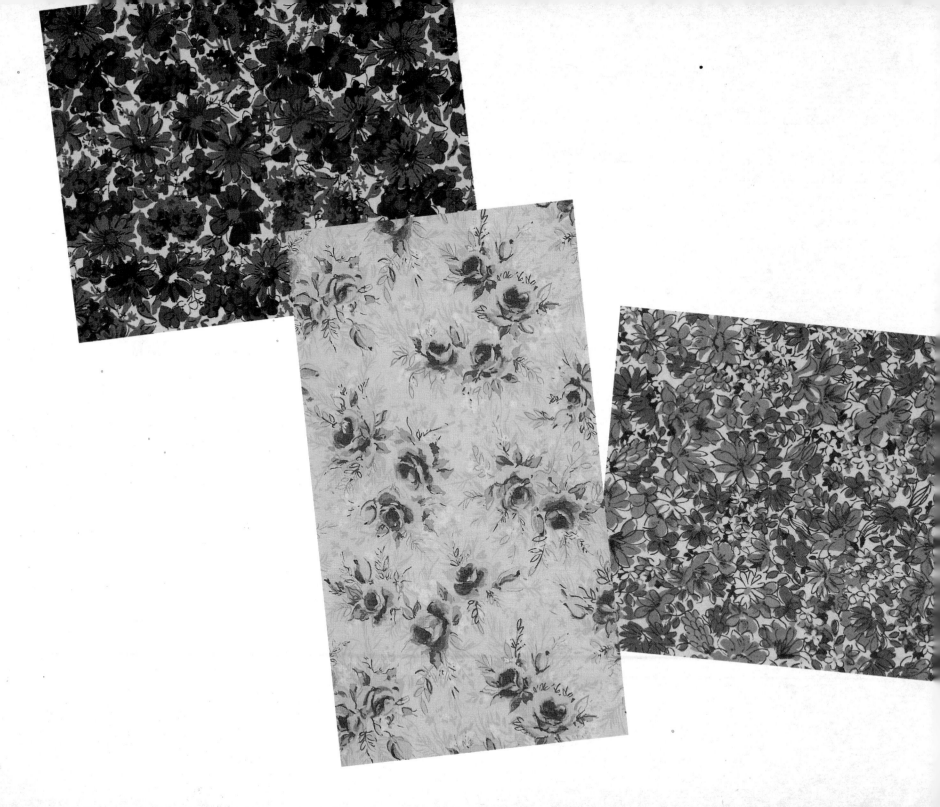

14

19

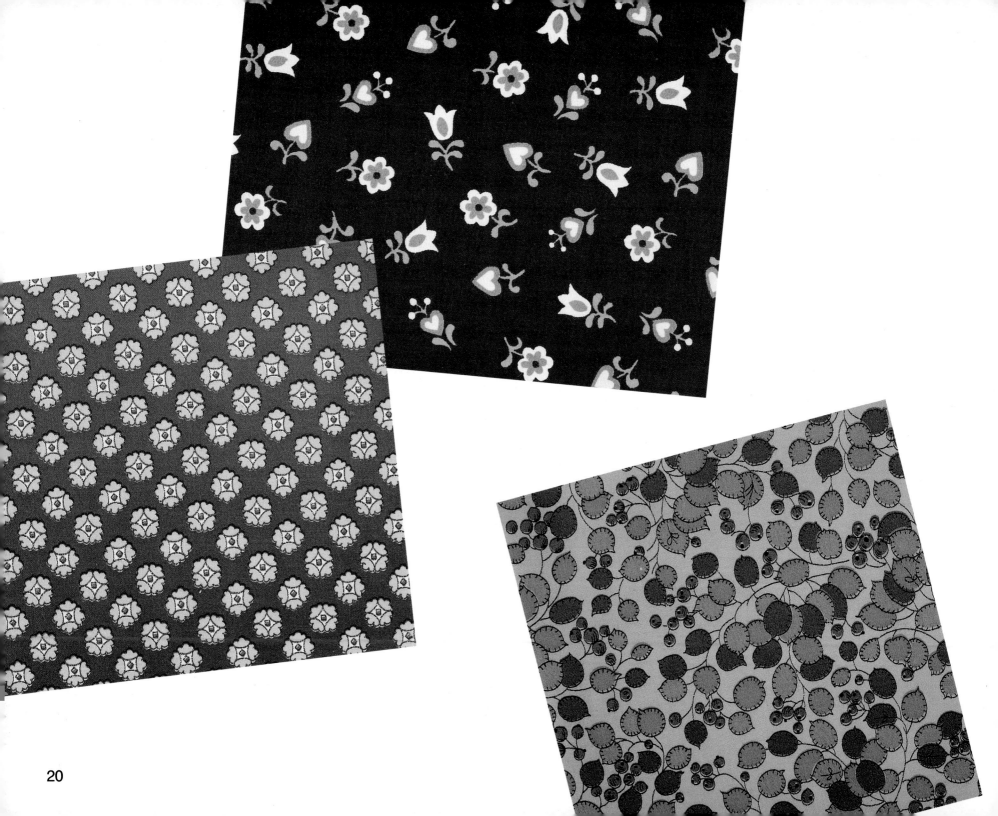

20

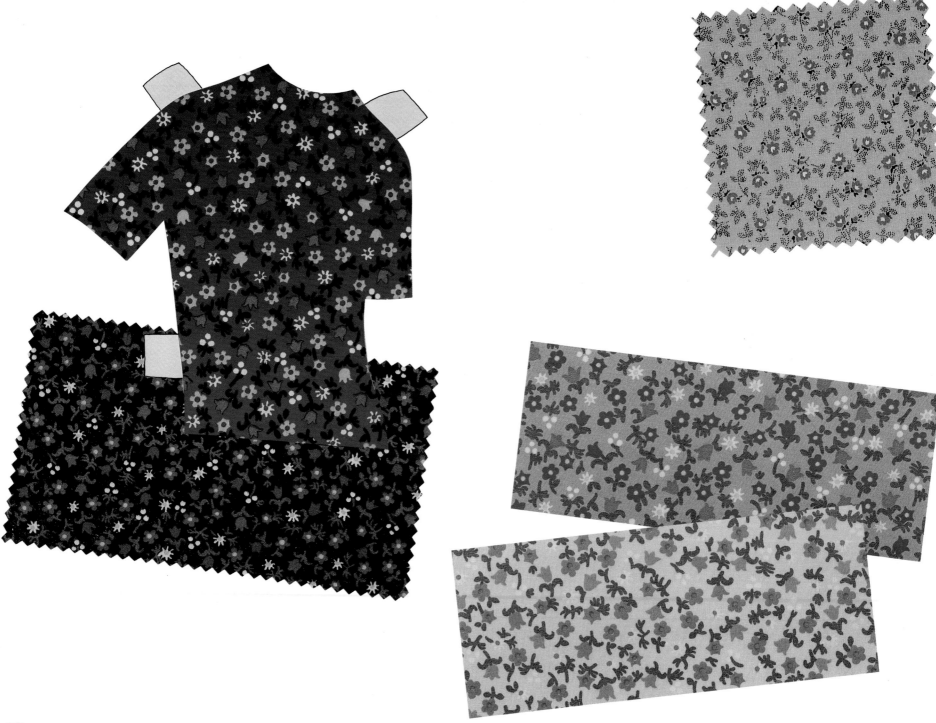

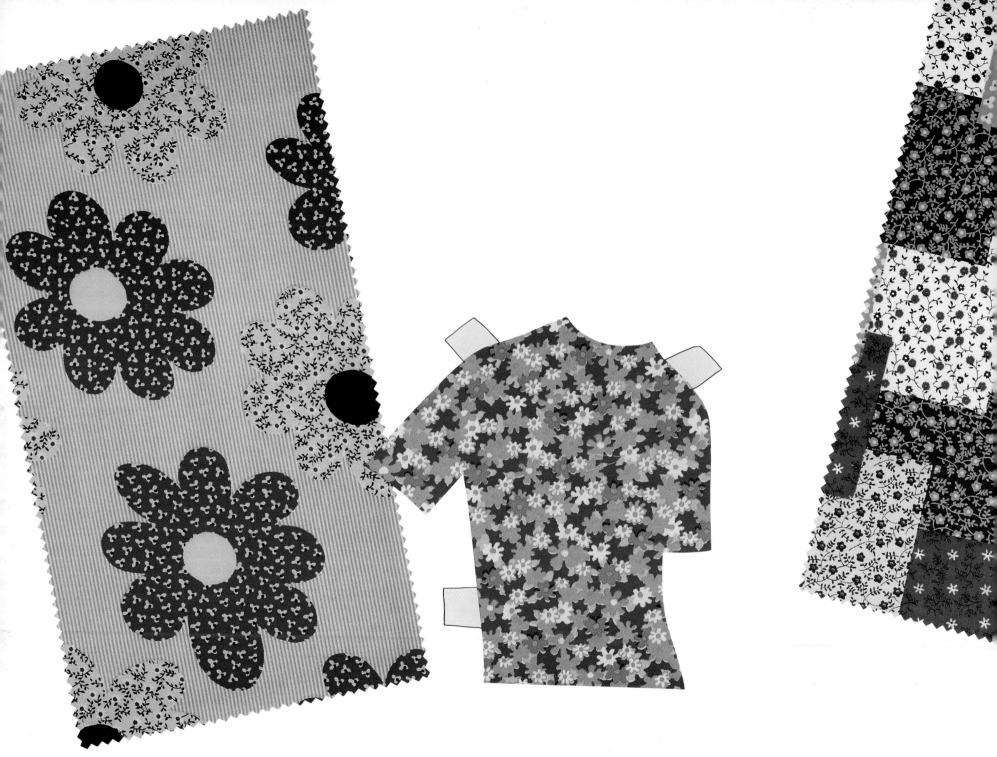

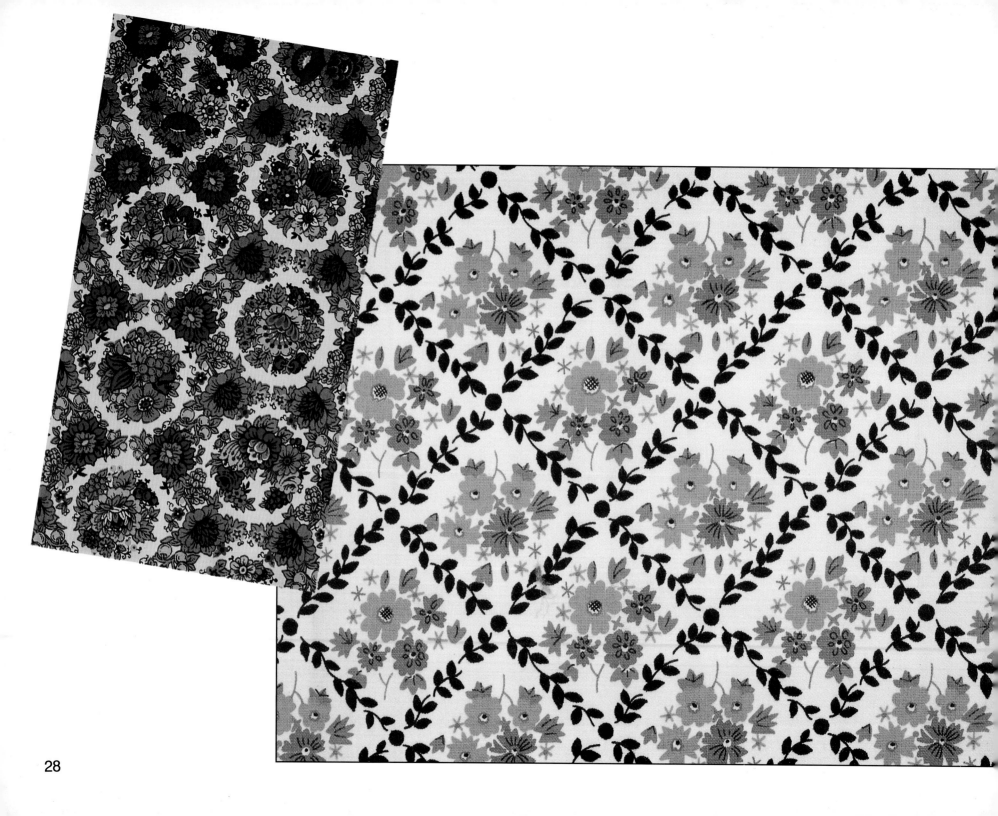

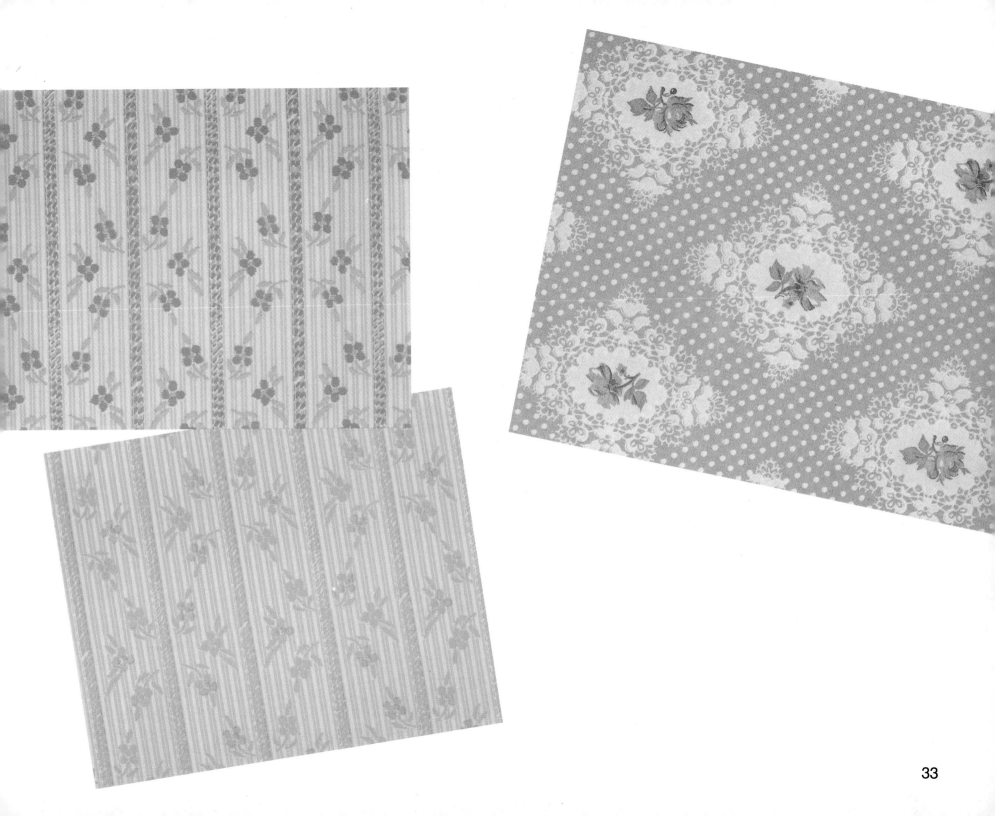

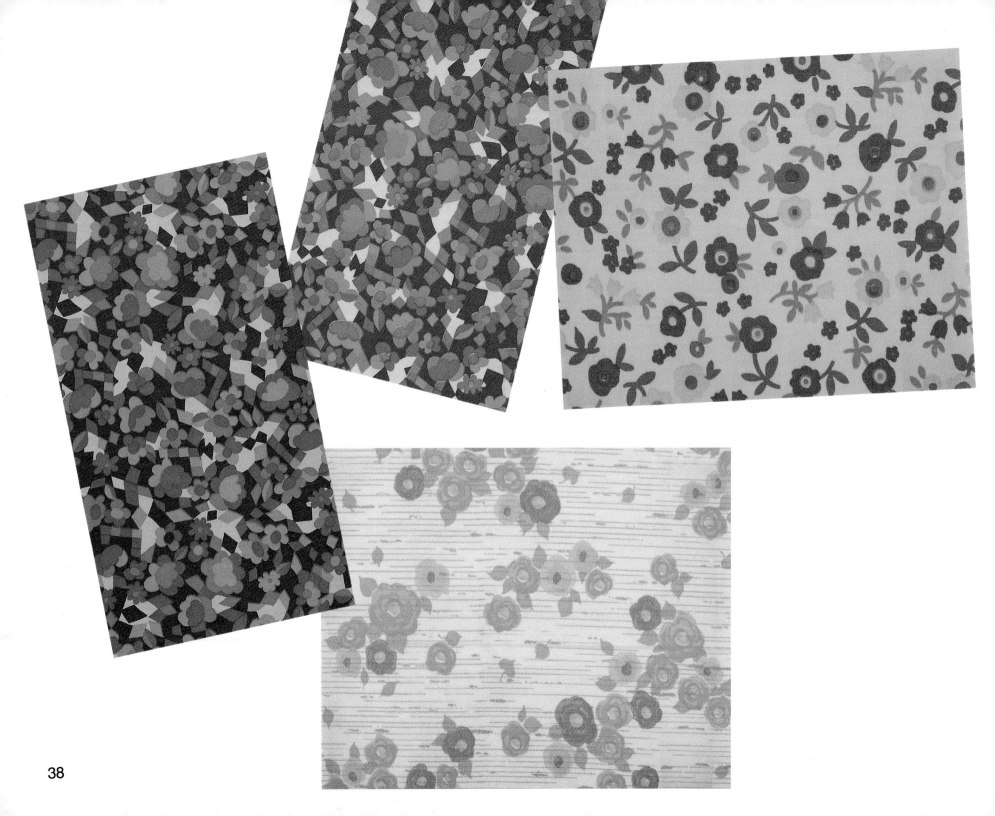

GROOVY GEOMETRICS

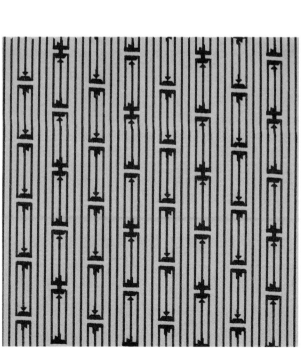

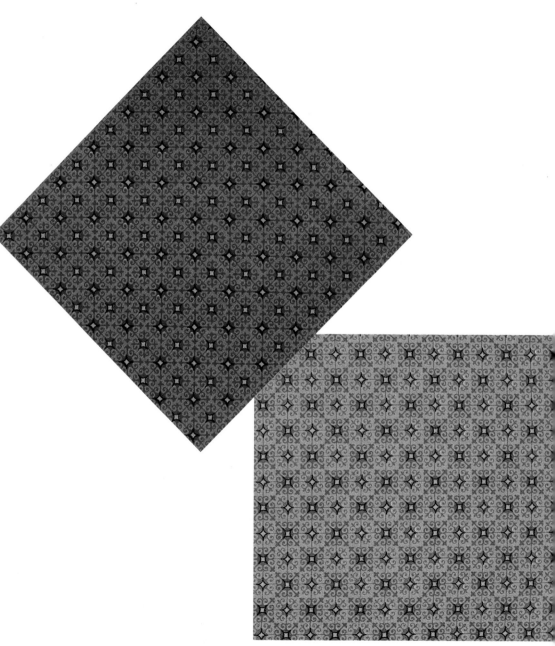

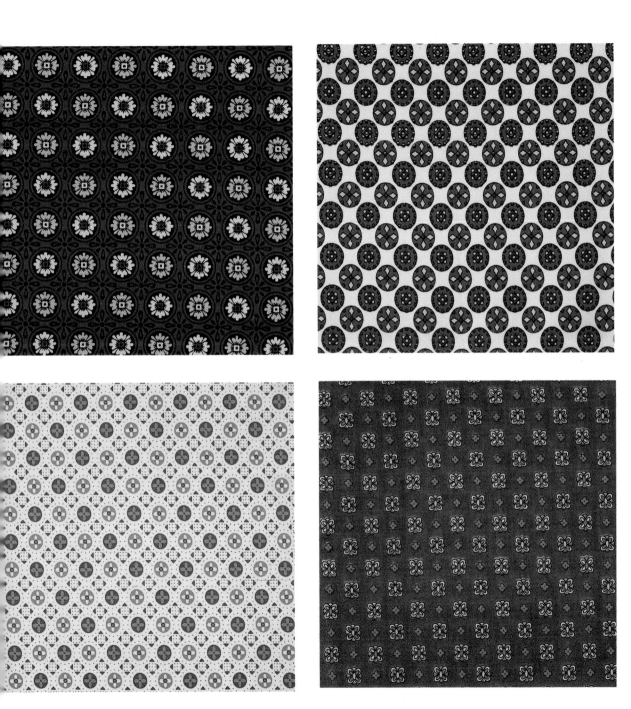
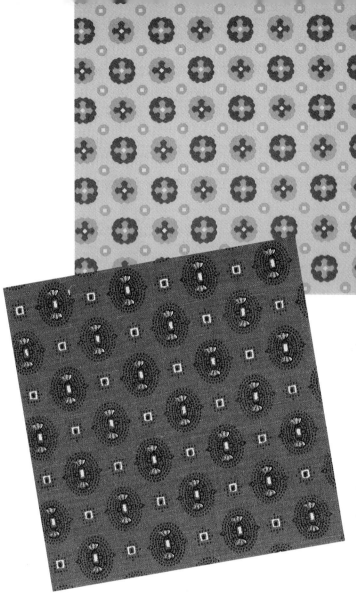

41

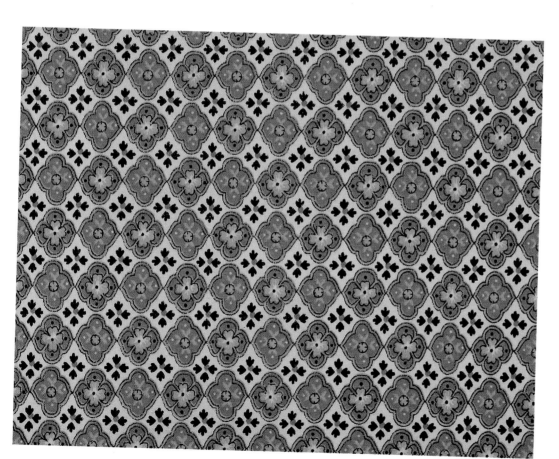

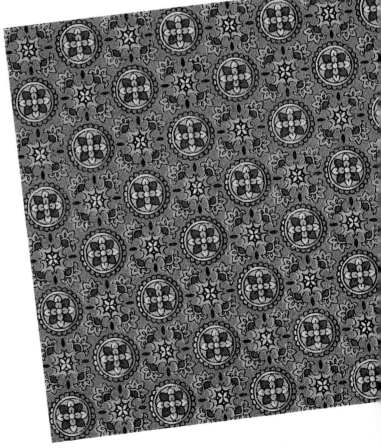

45

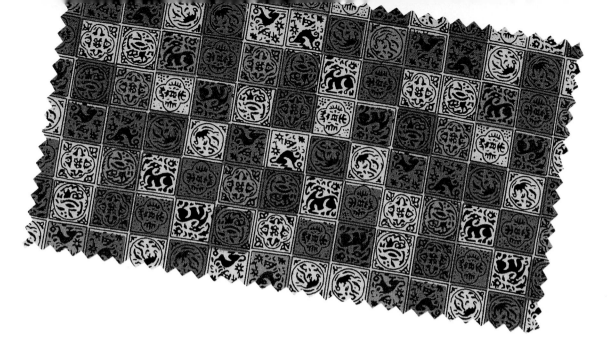

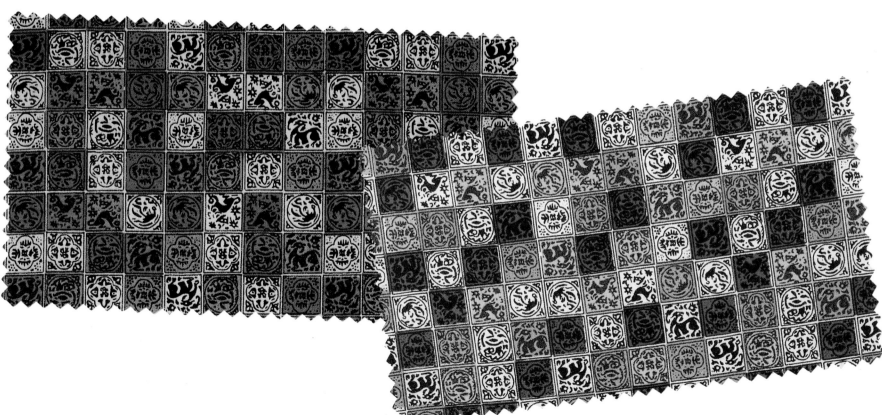

47

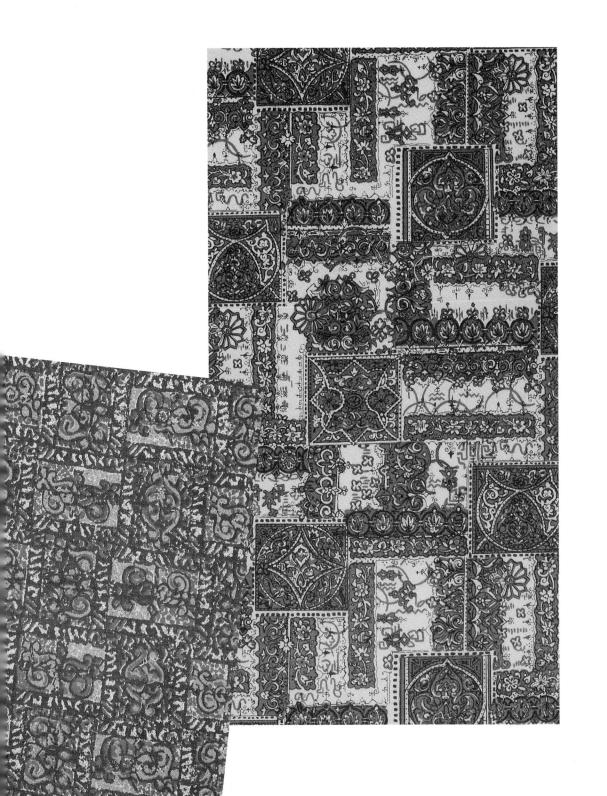
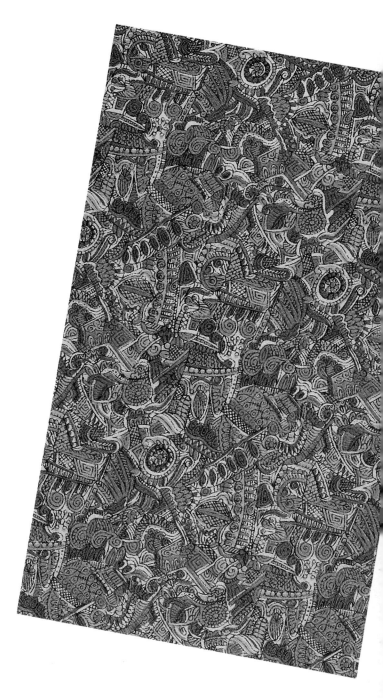

50

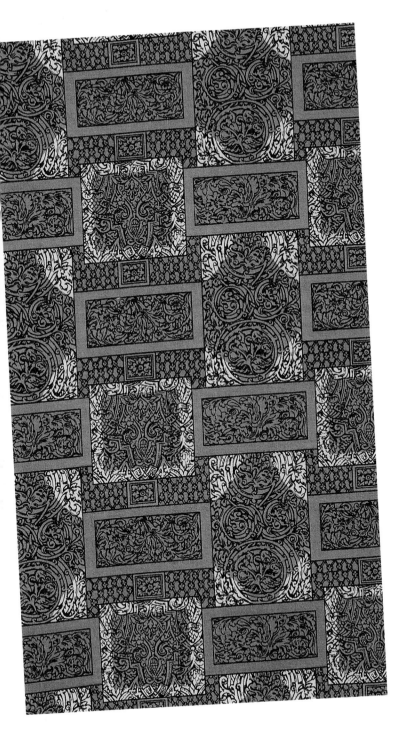

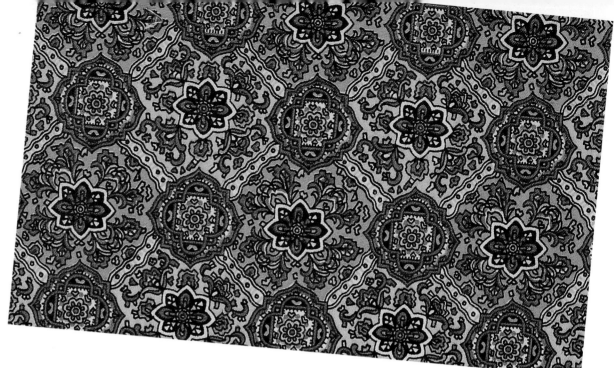

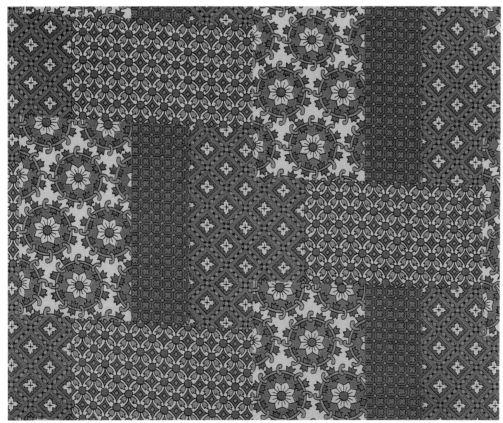

54

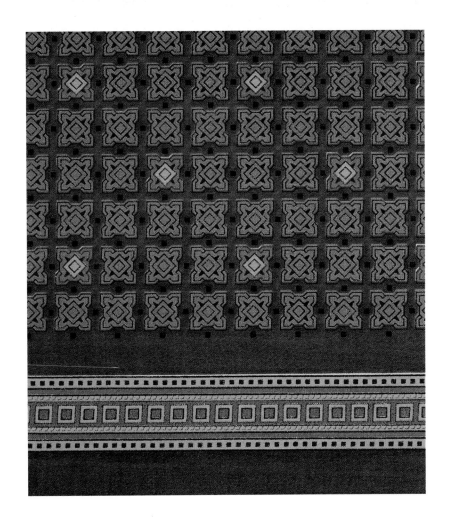

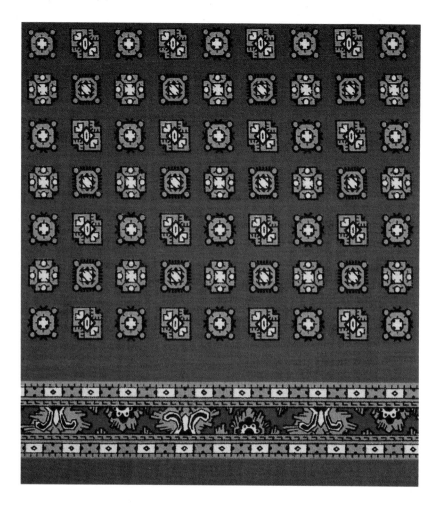

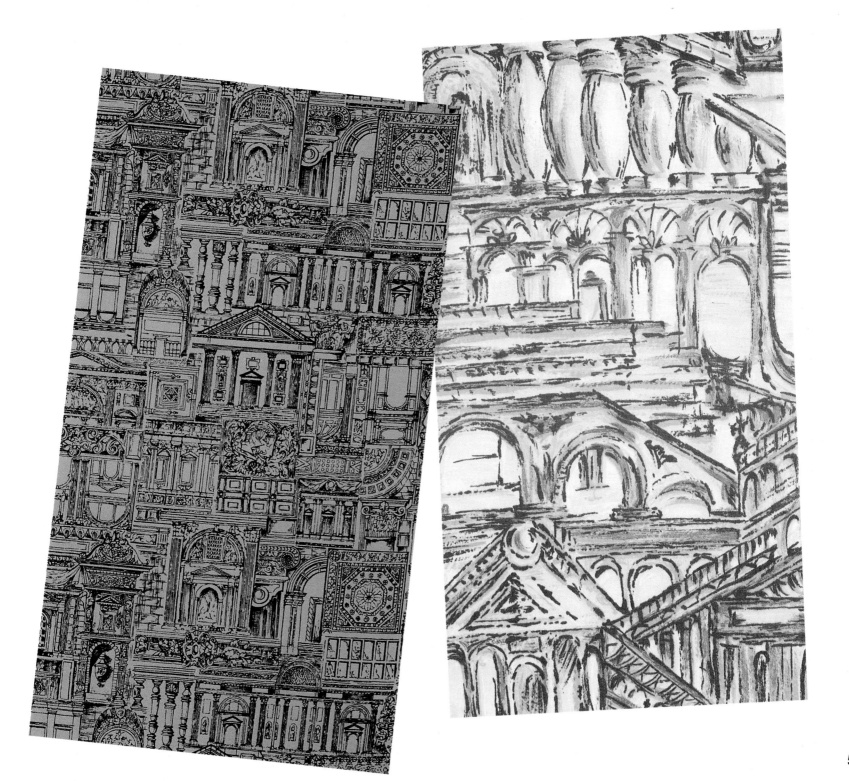

58

BOSS BORDERS

IT'S MY PAISLEY
AND I'LL WEAR IT
IF I WANT TO...

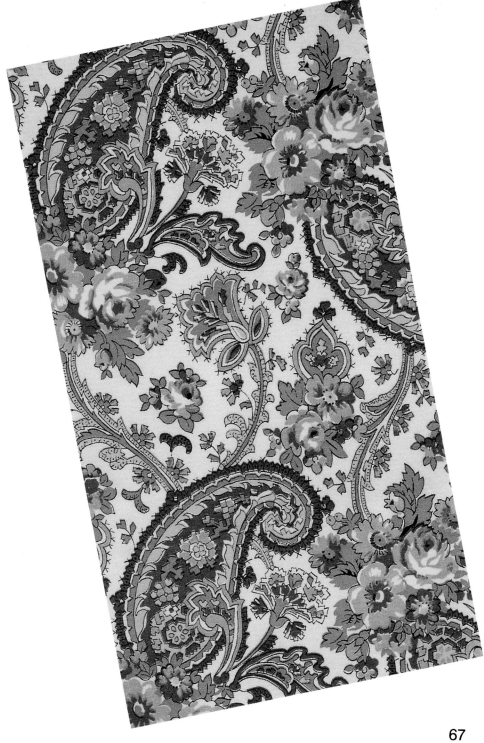

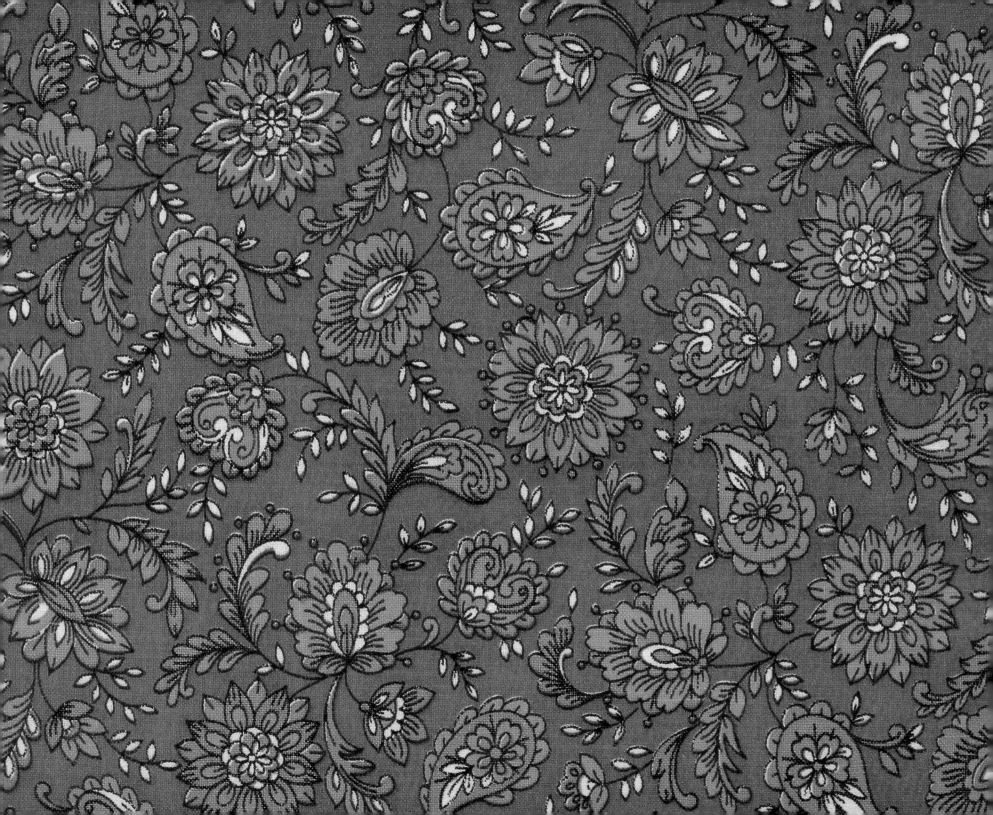

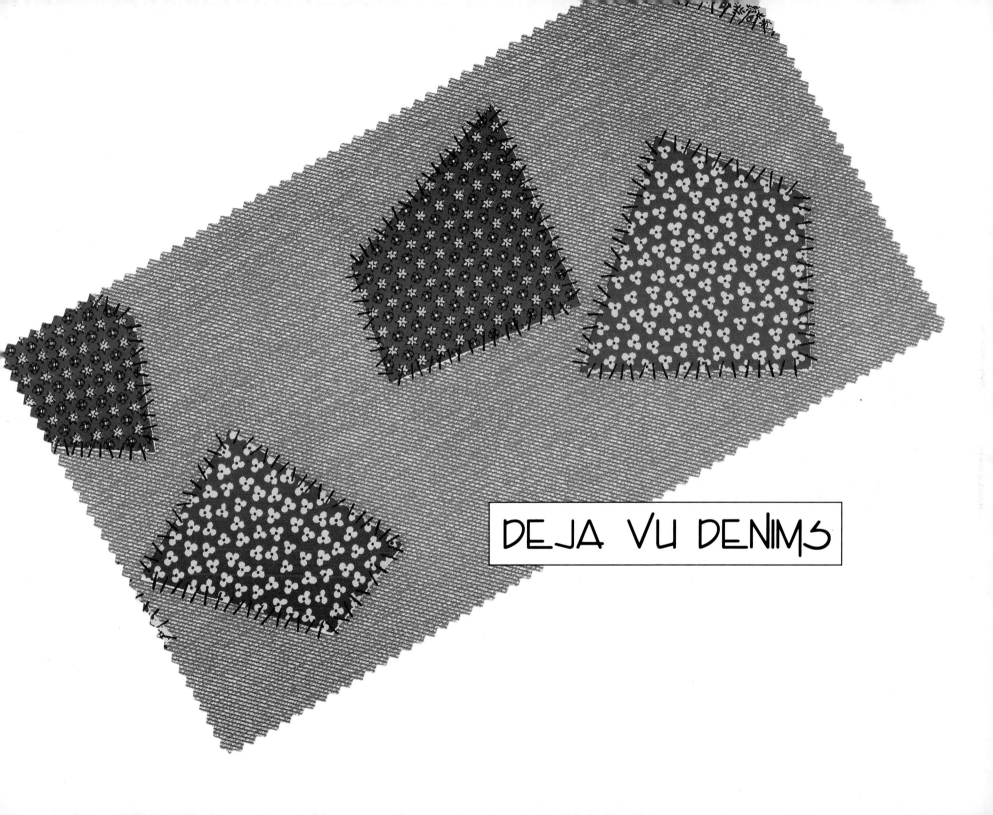

DEJA VU DENIMS

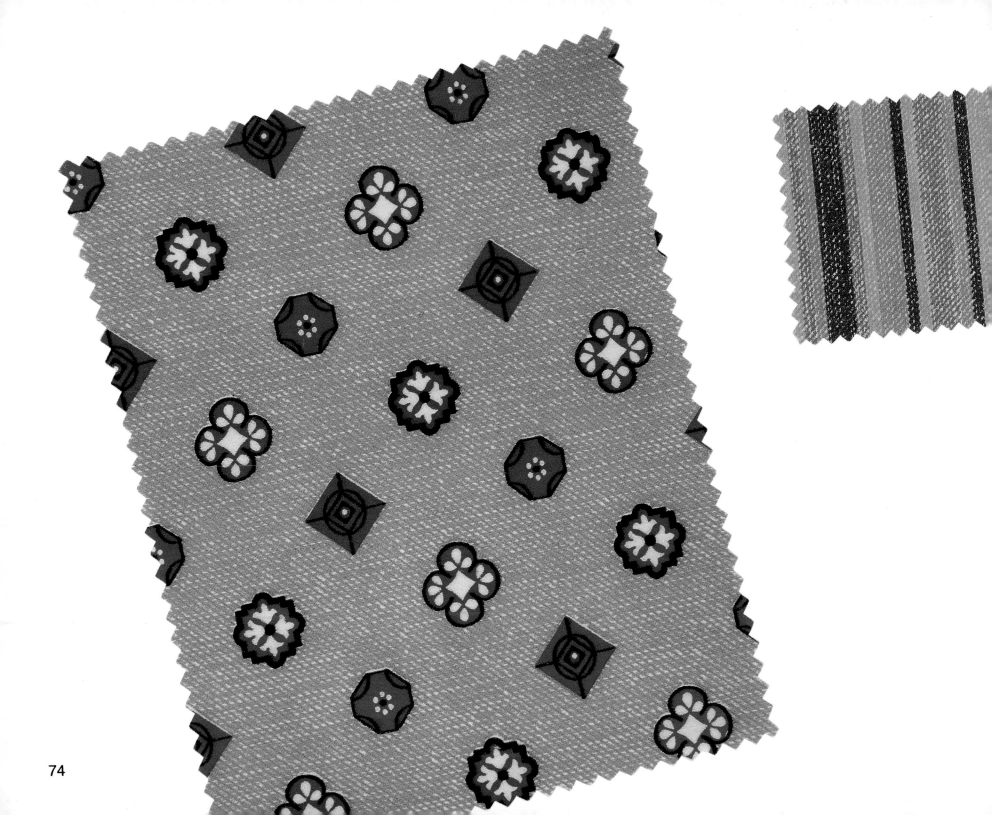

BANDANNA-NANNA-FO-FANNA

PILLOW TALK

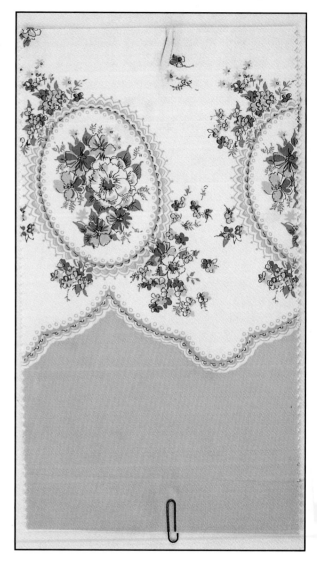

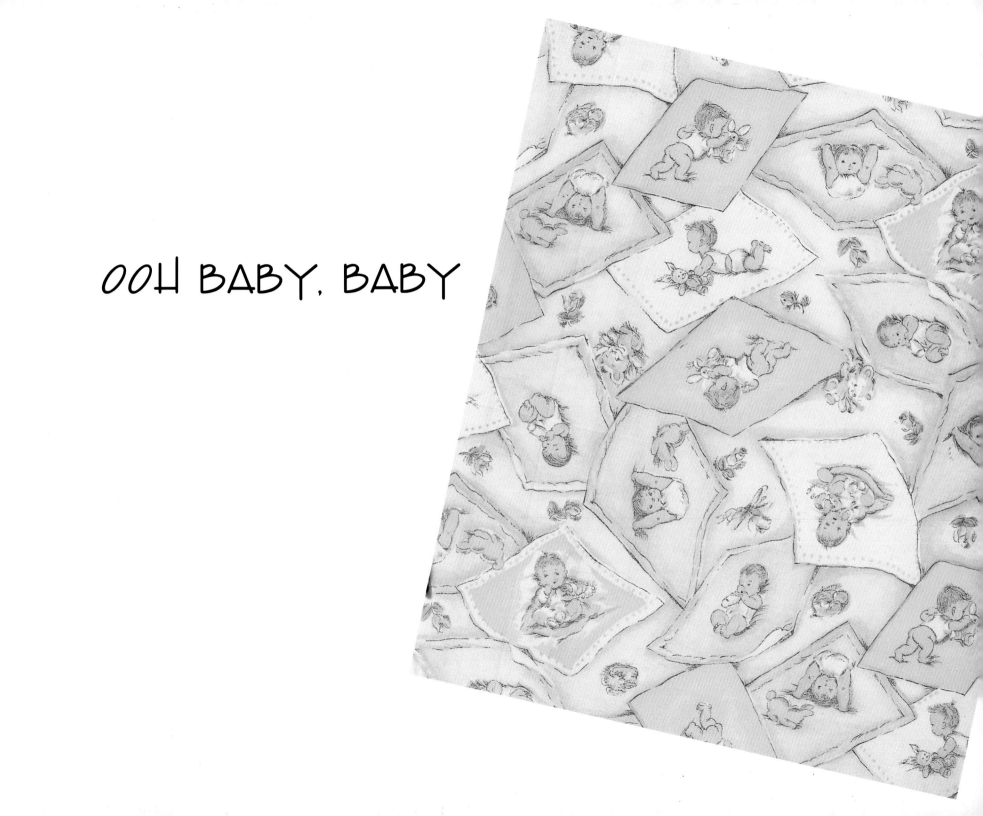

OOH BABY, BABY

91

HEY, GOOD LOOKIN'
WHATCHA GOT COOKIN'?

HOMEWARD BOUND

BRAND REGISTRY
WYOMING TERRITORY

⊡	BOX-T	⋀C	RAFTER-C
	WAGON TONGUE	⫶K	TUMBLING K
⟿	FLYING-W	⫐B	LAZY-B
⩘	ROCKING N	⊕	WAGON WHEEL
	BROKEN		

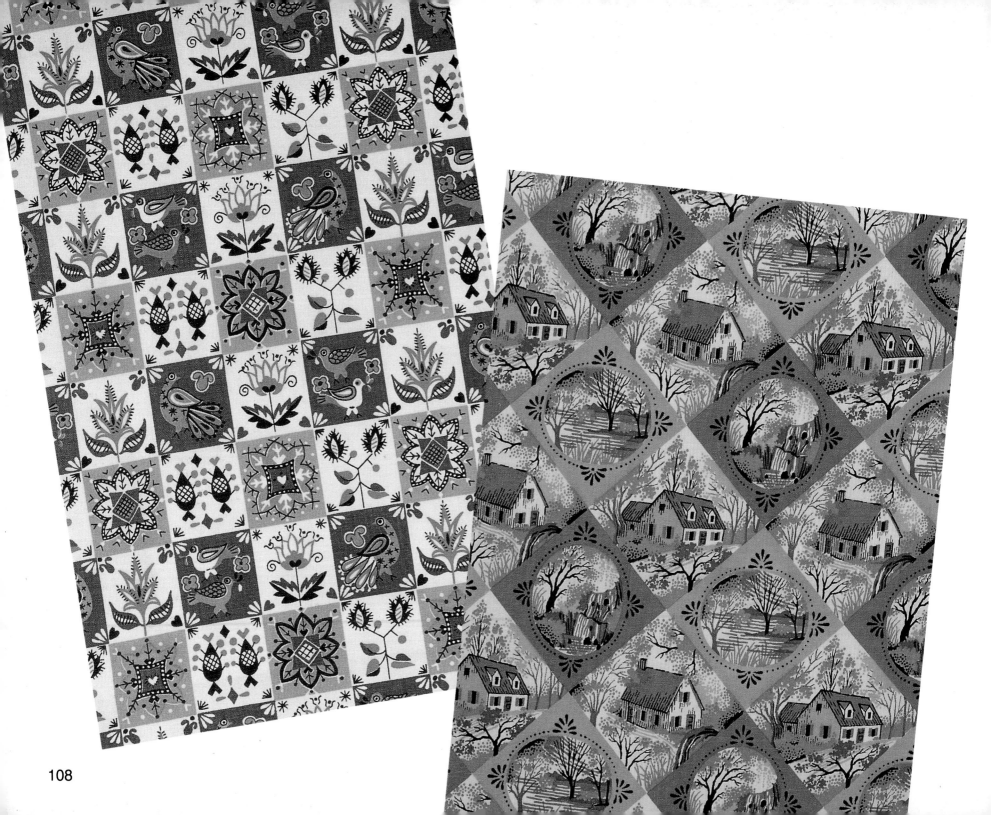

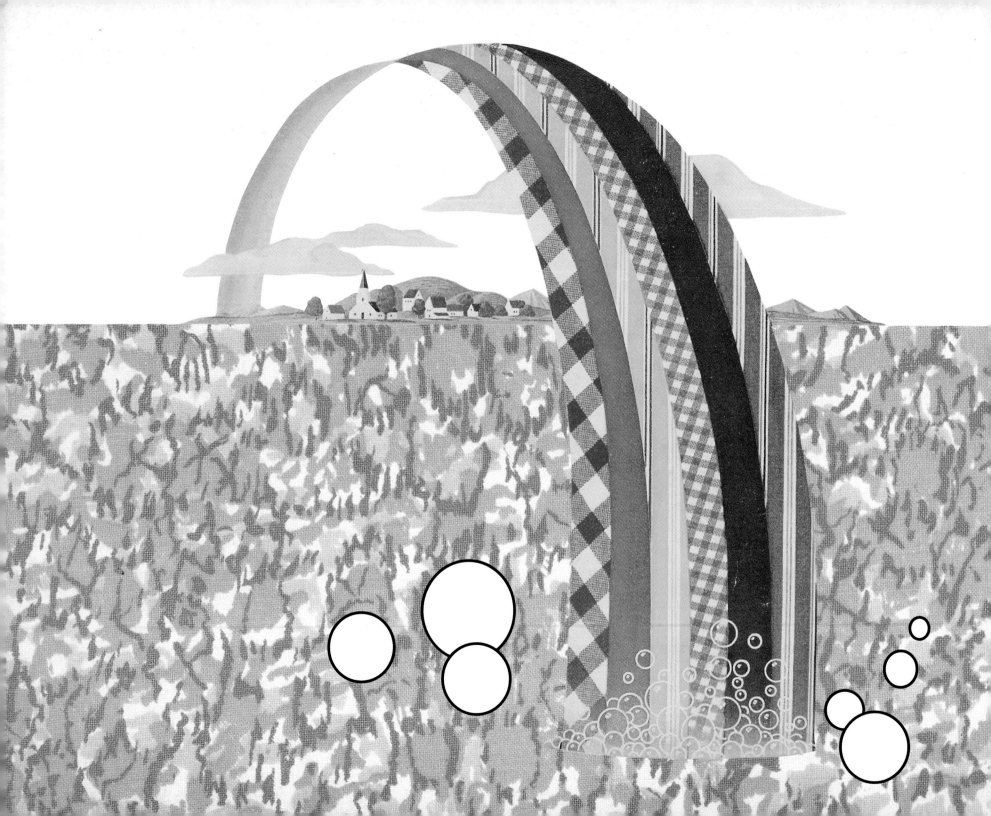